M000029306

A POET'S GUIDE TO THE BARS

KENNETH SONNY DONATO

PAX AMERICANA
PRODUCTIONS

Reprint Published by PAX AMERICANA PRODUCTIONS, 2011
Reprint Design: Fran Strauss; Edit: Jack Baxter
Photography by Michael Chieffo and Rob Neighbors
Cover photo: Rob Neighbors

Originally published by Illuminati Entertainment Group, 1992
Originally Designed by Mari Yoneda; Photography by Susan Maljan
Originally Edited by Carole Donovan and Caroline MacDonald

Copyright ©1992 and 2011 by Kenneth Sonny Donato

All rights reserved. No part of this book may be reproduced in any form,
electronic or mechanical, without written permission from the author,
except for brief inclusions of quotations for review.

Official Facebook Page:
A Poet's Guide To The Bars by Kenneth Sonny Donato

Dedicated to
Harry Dean Stanton
and
Mario Maglieri "The Pope of Sunset Strip"

Contents

INTRODUCTION

The bars that are
included in "A Poet's
Guide To The Bars"
all have a heritage.
They've been around
the block a few times,
so to speak. These
are the places where
dreamers, seekers,
searchers, schemers
go. They add music to
the night.

To the bars that serve
the night:
SALUTE!

KENNETH SONNY DONATO
HOLLYWOOD, CA

No Name Bar
(Yucca and Vine)

Bartenders are dueling
They deal through the night
Who cares if you're tired or lonely
Or old
Two shots in the night
First you're bought
Then you're sold
That's lonely
Last call
Who thought up that verse
Is that car a taxi
It looms like a hearse
I once drank with Chuck
It's Charles to you
With busted up knuckles
Bukowski
It's true
He once saved my life
Accident maybe not
It happened on Yucca
Don't bother to look
Scarred bearded face
Hands that shook
That was a good bar
The one with no name
He stood in that hallway
Alone in the hall
So lonely and dark
The only truth there
Came from his eyes
I swear
I was there
I reached for my knife
Not sure ➤

MICHAEL CHIEFFO

continued —

Unaware
He offered his drink
His last solitude
Ice melting
Blood brothers that drank hard
With nothing in sight
Just guys counting dreams
Comrades in the night

ROB NEIGHBORS

ROB NEIGHBORS

CODE – NO CODE

Early morning
Misty blue
Lone candlelight
In your eyes
One yellow rose
In your soul
Eyes that could pierce a locomotive
Eyes like that cold castle
We'd visit as children
With the old well in the back
We'd separate the wood
Over the well
Then drop a coin
Then listen
And wait
And wait some more
Then turn to leave
And laugh
While in the background
We'd hear a faint
But certain
Tiny
Splash
Eyes that deep
Two Cadillacs
Comin' through the midtown tunnel
With the high beams on
Eyes, my friend
That sleep under Rocky Mountain pine trees

THE FIREFLY

They closed that whore down
Stripped her of her dress
A hang bar
A snare
No better for worse
Straight shots
Dance on
Fire streaking
The right song
The right thing
Do it
Neon-streaked streets
A hooker or two
Wigs hung in windows
The Frolic awaits
Exhaust
Perfume
And lingo
Black leather on cowboys
A switchblade
A buck knife
Some pool sticks
Thirty-five reasons singing the same tune
CD juke
Heats up the night
Stones calling
On the street again
Cobalt paradise
A laugh
On the lam
A bartender somewhere
Comes out of the night
A neighborhood
Though not what you'd think
The strangest collection
Street smart
Incomplete

SUNDIALS

You became hope
As
Hope became you
Created in time
United by time
Until
Time shall be no more
On your side
Taken
By pride
Best friends reach out
In time
Connected faces
Departing glances
Romances
On the rocks
Counted out
In the third round
Hanging on the ropes
On the edge
Scared
Bared
In time
As time became hope

MICHAEL CHIEFFO

MICHAEL CHIEFFO

ELEVEN FIFTEEN
(THE FROLIC ROOM)

When cute becomes boring
The night turns to terse
The makeup's on bright
All girls are a nurse
Where nothing is normal
And something's not right
Where life's just a crapshoot
Let's hope there's a fight
The clocks can't keep up
We're moving too fast
Dreams in the stretch drive
Count sheep with a shotgun
Attached to your mouth
Chased down by a monster
We all call it fate
Wake up, man, you're sober
It's never too late
It all don't mean nothing
To no one outside
This warm tight circle
Of drunks that I've found
We're all chasing dreams
Outside of our hearts
It's Scotch on the rocks
A Christmas parade

BOOZE AND DUES

Booze and dues
Twelve-string guitars
Cigars
Kerouac guiding
Cassady trying
A bartender dazed
Infused with rage
Neon streaked
City streets
Taxi cabbing
Midnight stabbing
Death bars
Of bourbon drenched
Broken down
Stench
Lights up the night
Motorcycles
Hot dog stands
Hands
Pretzel vendors
Mortals dropping
Like goddamn flies
In summer's madness
Cigarettes smolder
A lonely tune
In the heat of the night
While scorpions death dance
At inseams in a heart
A neon juke
Becomes a best friend
Booze and dues
In the heat of the night

FELLINI'S

The car, she just lurches
A little too quick
The sound of those bikes, man
All falling as one
Some slob turns his head
You reach for the gun
It's nightlife
It squeezes your soul
Get to the next bar
Make that a big goal
Fellini's is looming
That smells
It's too loud
This place is too small
That guy keeps on looking
My pal's in the hall
That broad's eyes are scary
They dropped to my waist
I'd hate to see sunlight
Asleep on that face
Let's get in the car now
You owe me five bucks
He threw out my Cuban
My cool and my luck

TO MY ENEMIES

To my enemies, I give
A place in my soul
To my enemies, I give
Life's great turmoil
To my enemies, I give
Solitude of thought
That they
May
Someday
Know love
To my enemies, I give
All that they should ever see
Be it through jaded
Unequal eyes
To my enemies
I pray their forgiveness
That they should ever hold me
As their enemy
Wish that time's lonely cadence
Should ever be against their will
To my enemies
Sent without cause
A final salute

MICHAEL CHIEFFO

FIVE TO ONE IF YOU KNOW
(BARNEY'S BEANERY)

A sixties lead singer
He's brazen, he's bold
Slams gold in the corner
A ghost on a roll
Where pool is a test
The juke is the best
It's crusty charred burgers
Hot chili, red beans
A thousand old rules
You must eat in threes
The matches once said
"No fags allowed"
A vote in the council
An idea that's dead
If their hair ain't purple
Dyed black or obscene
What's that
On her head
It's hurting my life
Those boots are intense
Who made her so see
The wrong rock and roll flick
I'm glad it's not me
It ain't what they planned
Or wanted to be
It ain't what they dreamed
When they were all three
All right
In the daylight
There's no one around
There's pool mixed with laughter
A comforting sound

GRAY HOUR

Easy tricks stumble
On street corners
Glowing with history
Hipsters smile
At following footsteps
Soft rain
Eases world's blind rage
Razor-faced women
Lying to boyfriends
About last night
In morning's peaceful embrace
You sing
You confess
To whatever it is
We are one
I place my heart to you
Given from me
Free, Free, Free
At last
The end
Knocking its fateful
Tap, Tap, Tap
Life calls
Life hangs up
Life goes on

BUS STOP BAR
(SIDESHOW)

Ghost chasing
Lucid to the point
Sex in the walk-in
Backyard rendezvous
Laced vixens
Inside where they reach
Sweat-fuck her the hard way
Brain screamed
So it seems
She thought you were waiting
Who's fooling who now
Drink her last inhale
Gold green fishes
Slimmed down in the light
Shades of sunlight
Bursting rainbows
Through the cool morning waters
Eurasia in your cockpit
Life becomes what it is
All the time
Poets lose their cool
You wish
You get drunk
You do it all again
You do what is necessary
You return and never go back
You count dimes with your thumbs

THE EVERLASTING TRUTH

Watching the tide roll in
We begin
Freewheeling nomads
Count time
Throwing stupid rocks in buckets
While the waking world wonders
I spent time
Under Jersey boardwalks
Roots buried deeper than the eye can see
Alone but still standing
In no ones shadow
My friend
The Earth
Has it's own scent
Like highway tires whirring
Travel song of the wild
A child's dream
Answered in red clay dawns of peaceful desert
Where pain don't know color
Making sure there is a place on my fingertips
For ladybugs to rest their burden of grace
Provide hope, cheer
Things we hold dear
Futures
Uncharted
Deep tempered
Your sword I thee carry
In emerald azure
Aqua glazed
Amazed
While innocents tiptoe
After lingering echoes in morning's sweet madness

MICHAEL CHIEFFO

ROB NEIGHBORS

Rocking R
(The Roxy)

Hard rocks
Cold rolls
A closed door or two
Hiked up nylons
Guitar whiplash sex
Lips sliding down
Locked in bathrooms
A long hair attack
Bent over
Moaning, grinding
Cat calling
Two five-o-twos
Daughters
Giving what they got
Screwing, shampooing
Call you in the night
Fame on a doorstep
A smile
Faraway eyes
Hustle all the time
Scotch and teased hair
Tanqueray gimlets
Life without care

THE WAY IT GOES

Otis
Walk of life
Redding
Singing songs
For the ages
To shake hands
Clues
Ideas
Teaching
Time honored tunes
Sung from docks
On ageless bays
A vision appears
Right on time
Fed line by line
To the waiting
The wanting
The hungry of heart
Speaking in their own language

THE TROUBADOUR

A wooden dream bar
The bar of the stars
Shining in its own light
Coming and going
Maybe the road again
The clubhouse
Where the creators
Hang down
Built on a sound
That came from a heart
The pirate ship
Sails into waters
No man has seen
Things never change
Without reason or rhyme
Just hanging out there
Was like doing time
The kind you don't choose
It just came our way
For all to get on
A train ride
Into the heart of American music
And we all rode for free

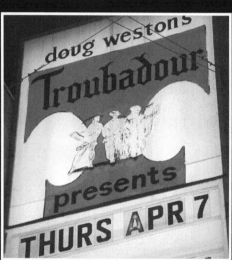
MICHAEL CHIEFFO

MICHAEL CHIEFFO

MICHAEL CHIEFFO

A Thousand Six Months

Schooled
By everlasting
I.Q. grasping
Over sexy
French poodles
Locked
In hot cars
All day
Some dog
Tied to a parked car
That's what
You call life
I don't want it
Standing proud
For what we are
Saying, feeling
Celluloid reeling
Here's to you
I love you
If I don't get
A chance
To say it again
It doesn't mean
It isn't so

CORONET

Inside
Footprints all over
Drunken cowboy boots
Praying they're not staying
You dream
Hard against the wind
Score jive
P.S. high school girlfriend
Skirt powder
Carnation
Bubble gum
Over and over
Mug love
Sam and Dave
Soul
Same Cooke and Ray
First feel sensual calling
Radios over bridges
Mixed up
Wild as you go
Twisted and driven
A slut for the night

THIS TIME

Best friends
Felt a voice
Ring, rang, sang
Tunes of vision
Bad boys without a cause
Trying to make it
All make sense
While nothing
No one
Says or does
Changes
Yes
The way you think
Times they all talked as one
A light shone the way
We all were seeking
Not what you'd think
Dreams are meant for dreamers
I saw roses
Drooped in pain
The kind
Money can't hide
Eyes that told stories
Hunger and the things you never knew
Bees wanting
A tune
Making springtime count
Like unsuspecting
Wild eyed innocents
Seeking
What we call our own
That day came
Knocking ➤

ROB NEIGHBORS

continued —

Now
In the depths
Of life's lonely recall
Making us all wince
In time-honored agony
In the distance
Stands our friendship
A toast
Offered within the boundaries
So to speak
A time to reflect
Hard edges on soft ideas
An ear for the givers
A heart for the takers
And, maybe someday
Angel baby
Love could look you
Right in the eyes

MICHAEL CHIEFFO

ROB NEIGHBORS

PARADISE BAR
(MURPHY'S)

Pool tables and dust
Shot glass beer joints
Stories told over pizza crust
You can't trust
Old guys sitting
At life's quiet corner
Cement mixers
Maudlin hipsters
Money making
Shaking
Artists
Sailboat rigging
Clam digging
Song singing comrades
Writing
Street fighting
Glistening eyes
Meet
Well kept ties
Sposin' I could see
Places You and Me
Could call our own

TWO RUN TRIPLE

Saints and sluts
Blood, rust
Indian cuts
Switchblade wielding
Power gliding the night
Bent and driven
Not forgiven
A Lou Reed song
Stalking alleyways
Dense fog
Drifting
Memory sifting
Pages ripped
Introverted, at best
Manic depressed
Manifest
Destiny, razors slashing, crashing, dreams
Landing
Razor face peering
A cab ride
Towards the enemy
Lit hallways
Rats on wires
Chirping the night
Give it to me
Given from you

DOUBLE ZERO
(CATHAY DE GRANDE)

Long shots, there are many
Odds don't include fate
Jukebox music
Diamond Dave and Top Jimmy
Skid marks on speed bumps
Life in L.A. bars
And we're all great stars
We star in our dramas
Conceived
Wrapped in gold
We're all pushing forty
While still stuck in first
You'll live
Then you'll learn
A silver cloud
Singing rain songs
Pine trees that whisper
A song in the night
Slut chasing
Home basing
You lead or you follow
Or live like a sheep
A vision of death
Appears on a horse
Swaying
Streams of sunlight callout your name

MICHAEL CHIEFFO

MICHAEL CHIEFFO

QUEEN OF CLUBS

Lost heartbeats in heaven
Know where to look
Autumn leaves
Rest on hard ground
You stoned my soul
I awakened
In a dream
Strive, survive
Play it live
Life's a surprise
Life is bold
Life is brave
Life ain't a march
To your waiting grave
Straight shot lent
Spent
Woman you love
Stretched out
On hospital's last death bed
While all that you see
Goes down in seconds
You wonder
Why
You think
Cry
Then never look back
It ain't me
It ain't you
Nothing you do
Brings her back
Mad, taunted
Sad, haunted
Life's promise
Calls out
To deaf ears
Reach out
Calm graceful night

RAINBOW

People
Searching the night
Life in a purse
Hanging around
Staying tough laced
Scarred on your ass
Are we there yet
Turn right
The Roxy
The head of the snake
She winds on through
She strip teased you
Where guys look like girls
And girls look like sluts
Music that moves you
Brits with haircuts
Take walks in some hall
Lipstick and leather
A hair show going down
Cave-lair of the rockers
Rainbow-gold
They're Tina and Tommy
A Vince
David too
Who got here first
Our pizza is due
The heat's in the kitchen
Mexicans on missions
Rock star Blitzkrieg
Cokin'-jokin'
Ray soakin'
Life as a stage
The last on the Strip

SHOW ME

Human eyes
Candlelit jazz
Sways
Softly in background
Black underwear and ankles
Slung over backs of sofas
Cathedral ceilings
Ocean fog drifts
In timeless state
Singing sad red rose songs
Out on the highway
Stretching in grey hour dawn
Heroes and women
Embrace
The gift of the day
While sipping
Someone else's coffee cup
Waiting for the train
Glorious and free
Rolling over the breezy fields
Making all the stops
The local weaves
Past the cornfields and plain houses
Hopeful eyes await the dawn
Peering over tips of mountains
Not yet climbed
Crystal light
Caught in the glimpse of an eye
Swallowed by the sound
Only a friend can make

ROB NEIGHBORS

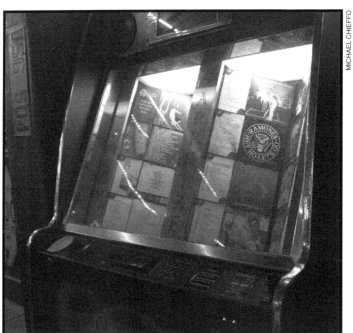

MICHAEL CHIEFFO

PORTS

Car search the street
You parked her last night
Along with your friends
So strong and so true
Just how did this slut
Wake up next to you
Don't wake her, you asshole
You hungover fool
You make up a game
Then ask for the rules
She's vampy
A real bitch
All wrapped up in verse
A life in a swallow
Posers and vixens
Where black is a law
Where big men insist
You look good at some door
Vampires that squawk
Walls that could talk
The bikes are out front
In Chartreuse and rain
Baby love on a juke
An acting bartender
Acts like a best friend
Jacques standing in the corner
Some gold in his hand
Makela in view
An early curfew
Actors with new rules
Sold on being cool
You wait to go piss
Some hallway called bliss
It feels like New York
Because you're not there

JUMPING FREIGHT

Now that I got here
I want to go back
Jumping boxcars
Out of East St. Louis
Rhythm of freights
Rolling
No local two-blocker
No street song
You bet
Summer graces
Faces
Warriors on leave
From their senses
Woe to the hand that sheds blood
Be it ours
Be it yours
Now that I got here
I want to go back
Faces made out of firewood
Smiles that come off Oriental vases
Strange music
The kind loneliness makes
Feathers
Real for the first time
Store bought clothes
Attached to your back
Woe to the hand that sheds blood in this house
This house we call home

ROUND AND ROUND
(THE CIRCLE)

Is there just a bar
Like ones we once knew
Where dogs were all right
Have you got a clue
Why that guy is angry
His pants are too tight
Patsy Cline on the juke
Jambalaya all night
It's hard boiled eggs, sawdust and cue balls
It's baldheaded Vets
They sell coke in the hall
Sometimes it's Jackie or Bonnie or Gypsy
The smell of the moment
It seizes your soul
There's Waylon and Roses and people who quit
An argument waiting
Just waiting for two
An after breakfast joke
That used to be you
You ain't got no future
No past
Only now
It's life on the lam
It's eggs cooked with spam
At least we could walk
Back home from this place
They call it The Circle
We'll see you around
Hard edges on softness
This place ain't so tough
Don't push that drunk slob
His beard is too rough ➤

ROB NEIGHBORS

continued —

The women are jaded
As cold as the wind
That slips in the bathroom
That creases your skin
It's all a surprise
A song you can't buy
Don't let them see fear
Appear
In your eyes
It's something not spoken or written or
sung
Is that bump on your waist really a gun
Could buy something legal or not
So it seems
You never see sunlight
Not even in dreams
There ain't no place left
Where we could just hide
Is that our cab calling
Let's go for a ride
That Scotch bit my heart
But it sure felt great

THE FORTY SOUTH COCHRAN AVENUE

Swollen drunken faces
Scan
Smoke-stained mirrors
At life passing by
Bells toll for the dead
Inside
Crashed out binges
White horse glides
Divides
Grey black shadows
Chasing myths
In Kansas cornfield
Full moonbeams
Illuminate the future
Counting stars
A ghost enters
A spirit takes control
Eagle swoops
Lizard waits in sun's blaze
Amazed
At not knowing nothing

MICHAEL CHIEFFO

MICHAEL CHIEFFO

CASABLANCA BAR
(BOARDNERS)

Watch out where you sit
Some guy spilled his beer
It's piled up ashtrays
Heroes and sneers
Switch-hitting women
With shiny black hair
An off-duty cop
They make up this lair
Perfume in the bathroom
An angry old matron
Things that you find
In any bus station
The broke and the weary
The hip and the cool
They pose and they drink
Some even shoot pool
A town with no heart
Just fortune and fame
A thousand of those
Whose life is a game
A bar of distinction
Just look at its face
All frayed and battered
It's fun and it's drama
It's life
It's forlorn
The joke of the game
It soon becomes clear
That drinking just stuffs
It crams all your fear
Like Bogie and Lauren
The bells they will toll
Although we've heard many
A chilling last call

SNOW ANGELS

Snow angels melt
In afternoon innocence
Reaching out
To knowing eyes
Fear grips soul
Then listens
Then waits
Love songs over radios
In spring's restless debate
Twenty-second bar fights
Linger on
In night's dark alley of fear
Dawn's misty surprise
Enters cross country boxcars
Songs meant for dreaming
Go down on highways
Wind blown spirits
Sent through doors
Pine trees and folklore
Tickets for speeding
Lawyers and whores
Midnight dances with bartenders
Demonic devices talking
Walking
Twisting fate
As snow angels
Reach out
To knowing eyes

BLUES TIMES TWO

In the heat
On the road
In blue jeans
Blues written for the lonely
Dreams that come true
Precious times two
Next to you
Counting the things
We used to do
Believing in no one greater than you
Conceived in late night's dreamy demure
Between the here and now
Dreams resting on your doorsteps
Naked paper
In this world
From within came the end
Door knocking rhymes and visions with dimes
Seven chances taken left that poor bitch shaken
Out of control
Susceptible by nature

MICHAEL CHIEFFO

MICHAEL CHIEFFO

SIXTY THOUSAND STRONG

My friend the rock star
Has busted eardrums
It's Chartreuse and coke
Heads that go hum
The Hendrix hotel
Where I'm coming from
Blood brothers that battle
The Venice Vampires
It's blood on your saddle
You scored in New York
With your junkie cheekbones
You're all wound up
Tight
Life in a red zone
You duck all contact
With things you don't know
You just struck out
Big time
Your life's being towed

ANOTHER GREAT F. POEM

Seeking
Truth from wandering minstrels
Coffee cups, porcelain, solid, reminders of days gone by
Glass stained with dreams from songwriters on edge
Beginning of end or end of beginning
Laid out solid
For all to see
Liaisons with strangers
Taking its toll
On life's turnpike to eternity
Lawyers don't charge drunken poets
For just trying to make it home
Streetwalkin' teenage girls spread the word
Making trash out of cash
Split decisions surround minds made up before getting facts
Mistrusting eyes
Tell lies to lovers
Chessmen stand
Waiting for honor
On boards made of wood
Coming alive
Sent to the end for what we call glory
Lead weighted baseball bats
Swung with hatred
Split skulls that don't move
Soft parades send inviting sounds
Bartenders guide drunken soldiers off to battle
Another pain-filled day

ODE TO GENE

A thousand to one
My friend
Lies peaceful
Asleep in the sun
Released without pardon
A song in a heart
Sung from someplace
Most men never know
An eagle spread wings
A little too high
A little out of control
America listened
Ears down
Twisted to railroad tracks
Dreaming of heroes
Dressed in their own colors
Some you never saw before
One-Eyed Jacks
Stand defiant and proud
Alone in the depths
Of night's sinful embrace
We tip our mournful hats to you
Hats filled with pride
Insights and joy

TWO SHOTS

Streetlights and late nights
They all start to wane
Like tired traffic signals
That just don't feel pain
It wasn't too late
Let's say just after dark
I heard two shots
Ring out in the night
I turned to see Jimmy, run out of the park
The screams
They grew louder
As time ticked his tune
The spring of his life
It was too much, man, too soon
Your soul starts to stagger
And life takes a swoon
Hey, Jimmy, you kiddin', you jivin', or what?
You shot that poor fuck, man
And what have you got?
We opened the wallet, in rain and the dark
Just pictures of daughters
A wife with a heart
Hey, Jimmy, you did him
You ended his life
When you pulled that trigger
You stepped on a dream
The rain, it kept pouring
A cadence in time
Streetlights and late nights
They all start to wane
Like tired traffic signals
That just don't feel pain

Dan Tana's
RESTAURANT
ITALIAN
CUISINE
COCKTAILS
doug weston's
Troubadour